IS IT FAR TO ZANZIBAR?

Nikki Grimes

IS IT FAR TO ZANZIBAR?

POEMS ABOUT TANZANIA

Illustrated by Betsy Lewin

LOTHROP, LEE & SHEPARD BOOKS • NEW YORK

I am grateful for a grant from the Ford Foundation, without which the manuscript for this book would not have been possible. —N.G.

Watercolor paints were used for the full-color illustrations.
The text type is 12-point Caxton.

Published by Lothrop, Lee & Shepard Books
a division of William Morrow and Company, Inc.
1350 Avenue of the Americas, New York, NY 10019
www.williammorrow.com

Printed in Hong Kong by South China Printing Company (1988) Ltd.
10   9   8   7   6   5   4   3   2   1

601 894488

LIBRARY OF CONGRESS CATALOGING-IN-PUBLICATION DATA
Grimes, Nikki.
Is it far to Zanzibar?: poems about Tanzania/ by Nikki Grimes;
illustrated by Betsy Lewin.
p. cm.
Summary: Over a dozen poems with some aspect of the African country of Tanzania as a theme.
ISBN 0-688-13157-3 (trade)—ISBN 0-688-13158-1 (library)
1. Tanzania—Juvenile poetry. 2. Children's poetry, American.
[1. Tanzania—Poetry. 2. American poetry.] I. Lewin, Betsy, ill. II. Title.
PS3557.R489982I69 2000 811'.54—dc20 96-2335 CIP AC

For Michelle Y. Green
because we speak the same language —N.G.

To fellow wasafari, Cynthia and Richard Trent —B.L.

IS IT FAR TO ZANZIBAR?

Down the Road a Bit

Walk down the road a bit, cousin.
Walk down the road a bit.
The place you're seeking isn't hard to find.

Go past the grove of pawpaw,
Go past the field of maize,
Go past the grasses where the young goats graze.

Go past the old men carving,
Go past the market stands,
Go past the tree with branches cupped like hands.

Now, when you hear the crickets,
You'll know you're almost there.
Take care, or you'll go too far down the road.

Walk down the road a bit, cousin.
Walk down the road a bit.
The place you're seeking, I will help you to find.

I Safiri

I *safiri,* you *safiri.*
Everyone is on safari,
even Godfather Omari
travels to somewhere.

He *safiri,* she *safiri.*
Off we go on *msafara,*
caravan to old Mombasa.
Lorries take us there.

Msafari, wasafari,
voyagers from Zanzibar, we
sail the coastline of the sea
and fish without a care.

Bus Ride

People jam the open door,
Bright cloth bundles crowd the floor,
Wailing infants at my back,
Beetles launching an attack,
Squawking chickens near my seat,
Billy goats sniff at my feet,
Cardboard suitcase on my knees,
Temperature ninety degrees,
I scream, "STOP! Bus driver, please!
Park a minute near those trees.
Let me off this bus right now!"
I'm sure I'll get home somehow.

Rainy Season

Aiii! The raindrops streak our faces.
All at once, the shower chases
creatures from their hiding places.
Five goats, four ewes,
three snakes, two gnus,
and one field mouse
squeeze inside my house!

Many Mangoes

A so-old man on a so-old bike
cycled down a coconut tree–lined street,
singing this simple song:

"Ripe and sweet, juicy meat.
A few shillings only for a tasty treat.
Mangoes, mangoes. Fruit of heaven.
Mangoes, mangoes. Buy six. Buy seven.
I saved the best for you."

Mount Meru

In Arusha, there's a mountain.
There's a mountain known as Meru.
First it's there, then disappearing.
Wrapped in mist, how it misleads you.

Is it real, or just imagined?
Are those clouds? Or snow-capped peaks?
Are those voices in the valley
or a gentle wind that speaks?

All is eerie in Arusha,
in Arusha on Mount Meru.
Men have vanished on that mountain,
legend says. But . . . is it true?

Home Visit

Malaika went home for a visit.
"*Habari,* Mama," she said.
Immediately her mother brought out
chicken, *ugali,* and bread.

Malaika went home for a visit.
Her sister stirred up a pot
of peppery stew with meat and rice.
Malaika said, "Why not?"

Malaika went home for a visit.
Her sister-in-law had made
a roasted lamb with mustard greens.
Politely, Malaika stayed.

Malaika went home for a visit.
Her cousin begged her to dine.
Malaika thought that she would burst,
but, smiling, she said, "Fine."

Malaika went home for a visit.
She was blessed with family to spare.
And everywhere Malaika went,
a meal was waiting there.

Malaika went home for a visit.
She'll do it again someday.
"Next time," she said, "I'll bring a friend
to help roll me away!"

Simba Nje Leo

"Simba nje leo!"
the gatekeeper said to me.
"The lion is out today
roaming wild and free."
Now *simba* roars and eyes me hungrily.
Moja, mbili, tatu.
I count from one to three,
then, swiftly as a panther,
I shinny up a tree. . . .
Tafadali, Mama!
Please rescue me!

Pilipili Hoho (Hot Pepper)

Pilipili hoho
makes the chicken hot hot!
I scoop *ugali* from the pot.
I know that it will take a lot
to soothe my burning tongue.

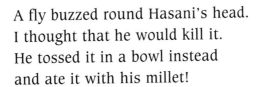

Snack Time

A fly buzzed round Hasani's head.
I thought that he would kill it.
He tossed it in a bowl instead
and ate it with his millet!

Picking Coffee

"We are all just picking coffee,"
said my grandfather one day.
"Every child born on this earth
must earn his way.

"We are all just picking coffee.
Everyone must do his chores,
whether planting, tending sheep,
or sweeping floors."

We are all just picking coffee,
but I'm glad there's time to play.
When I'm older, I can learn
to earn my way!

Haraka, Haraka

Haraka! Hurry! Right this minute.
Aina baraka. There's no blessing in it.
The elders tell me this each day,
but I *haraka* anyway!

I eat my porridge while it's too hot.
I scream and burn my tongue a lot!
I rush to fill the water pail,
then spill the water without fail!
I take my time at first, but then
I start to rush around again.

Haraka! Hurry! Right this minute.
Aina baraka. There's no blessing in it.
I hear these wise words every day,
but I *haraka* anyway!

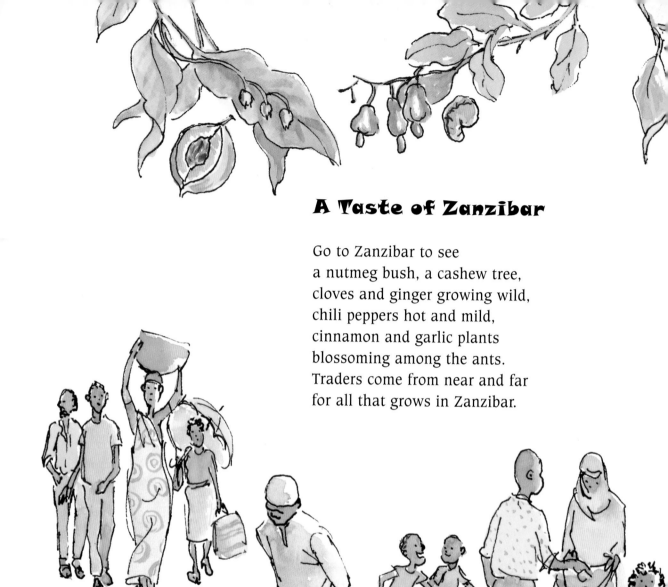

A Taste of Zanzibar

Go to Zanzibar to see
a nutmeg bush, a cashew tree,
cloves and ginger growing wild,
chili peppers hot and mild,
cinnamon and garlic plants
blossoming among the ants.
Traders come from near and far
for all that grows in Zanzibar.

VOCABULARY

Aina baraka (ahee-NAH bah-RAH-kah) There's no blessing in it

habari (hah-BAH-ree) hello

haraka (hah-RAH-kah) hurry

leo (LEH-oh) today

mbili (mee-BEE-lee) two

moja (MOH-jah) one

msafara (em-sah-FAH-rah) expedition

msafari (em-sah-FAH-ree) traveler

nje (en-JEH) out

pawpaw (pahw-pahw) papaya

pilipili hoho (pee-LEE-pee-LEE hoh-hoh) hot red pepper

safari (sah-FAH-ree) trip, journey

safiri (sah-FEE-ree) to travel

simba (SEEM-bah) lion

tafadali (tah-fah-DAH-lee) please

tatu (TAH-too) three

ugali (oo-GAH-lee) cornmeal

wasafari (wah-sah-FAH-ree) travelers

All the vocabulary words except *pawpaw* are Swahili. *Pawpaw* is a modification of *papaya*, a word of Native American origin. While now common in Tanzania, both papayas and maize (corn) are native to the Americas.

Lorries are trucks.

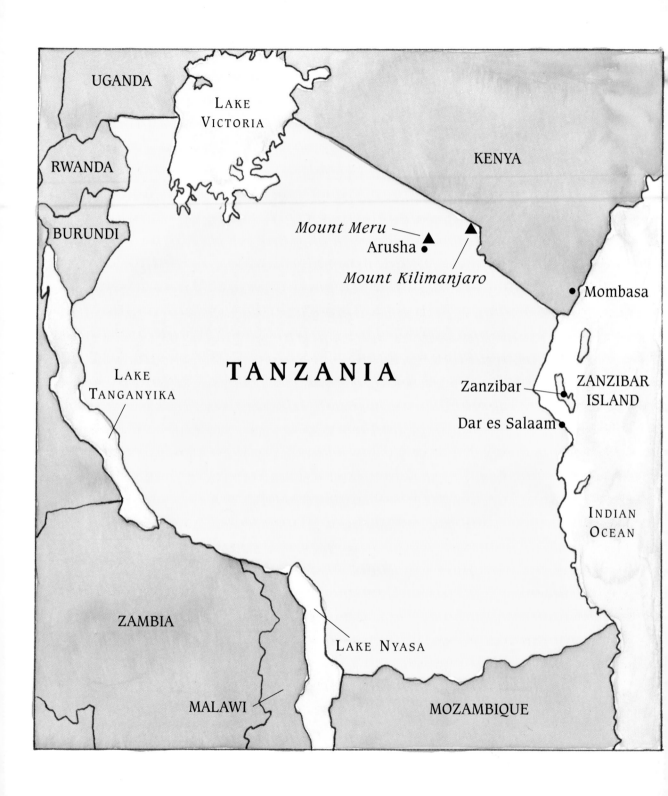

DATE DUE